THE OFFICIAL LITTLE BOOK OF

LIVERPOOL FC

FOURTH EDITION

An official Liverpool FC publication

EDITED BY
GEOFF TIBBALLS

CARLTON
BOOKS

First published by Carlton Books in 2002
Reprinted with updates in 2005, 2007
Second edition 2010, 2012
Third edition 2013
Fouth edition 2016

Carlton Books Limited
20 Mortimer Street
London W1T 3JW

Liverpool Football Club logo™ and © Liverpool Football Club
and Athletic Grounds Limited 2016

Text and design copyright
© Carlton Books Limited 2002, 2005, 2007, 2010, 2013, 2016

Photography © Liverpool FC & AG Ltd.

ISBN 978-1-78097-849-9

Printed in Dubai

CONTENTS

INTRODUCTION

Bill Shankly, Tommy Smith, the Kop – the history of Liverpool Football Club is rich in colourful characters who have never been short of a sharp one-liner. You only have to look at the number of ex-Liverpool players who have become TV pundits. To think, Alan Hansen was criticised by his former manager for not having enough to say for himself!

Alongside the shafts of Scouse and Scottish wit, this book contains more serious quotes offering rare insights into the private lives and careers of the players and management staff who have graced Anfield. So if you want to know what it means to join Liverpool FC, play at Anfield or what Bill Shankly really thought of Everton, read on.

CHAPTER 1

THE
LIVERPOOL WAY

66 When you have a Liverpool shirt on your back as part of the squad, you will do anything to make sure you preserve what it stands for. **99**

Gérard Houllier

"From my first day at Melwood,
I appreciated Liverpool's
special DNA.**"**

9

John Barnes

This record sums up our spirit on the field. No player in my team struggles or battles alone. There's always someone there to help him.

Bill Shankly

discussing 'You'll Never Walk Alone'

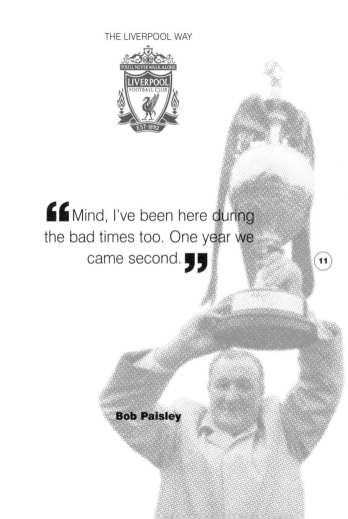

“Mind, I've been here during the bad times too. One year we came second. **”**

11

Bob Paisley

12

“Liverpool Football Club is all about winning things and being a source of pride to our fans. It has no other purpose. ”

David Moores,
Honorary Life President of Liverpool Football Club

" The only way to beat Liverpool is to let the ball down. **"**

13

Portsmouth manager **Alan Ball**

❝ There is no one anywhere in the world, at any stage, who is any bigger or any better than this football club. **❞**

Kenny Dalglish

"It's there to remind our lads who they're playing for, and to remind the opposition who they're playing against. **"** (15)

Bill Shankly

explaining the significance of the 'This Is Anfield' plaque

❝It was United's ground, mostly their supporters, but it was our ball.**❞**

Brendan Rodgers

after a resounding 3-0 victory at Old Trafford in March 2014

"You get to wish that they would just occasionally pass the ball to the other team, like the rest of us do.**"**

(17)

Watford boss **Graham Taylor** *despairing of playing Liverpool*

18

"The Liverpool philosophy is simple, and is based on total belief. Maybe that has been the key to Liverpool's consistency. We were taught to go out there, play our own game and fear no one."

Phil Neal

" Our methods are so easy, sometimes players don't understand them at first. **"**

Joe Fagan

" Anfield without European football is like a banquet without wine. **"**

Roy Evans

" Liverpool has always been about winning,
but it's also about the style. Over time we'll
look to put that in place at all levels. **"** (21)

Brendan Rodgers

❝It's a magical, magical feeling to walk on to this pitch and think that we are the new owners.❞

John W. Henry

stepping out at Anfield

"What attracts you to this club is its history. If you are clever and bright enough, you will look into the history.**"**

(23)

Brendan Rodgers

CHAPTER 2

SHANKLY'S
SAYINGS

" There are two great teams
in Liverpool: Liverpool and
Liverpool Reserves. **"**

Bill Shankly

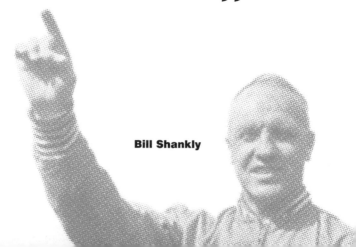

"If Everton were playing at the bottom of my garden, I'd draw the curtains.**"**

Bill Shankly

❝ Don't worry, Alan. You'll be playing near a great side. **❞**

Bill Shankly

to Alan Ball after he joined Everton

"I'm a people's man.
Only the people matter.**"**

Bill Shankly

30

66 Matt has got a bad back. I tell you it's two bad backs! And not much of a midfield either. **99**

Bill Shankly

putting the boot into Matt Busby's Manchester United

ff There's Man United and Man City at the bottom of Division One. And by God they'll take some shifting. **JJ**

(31)

Bill Shankly

looking at the League table early in the 1972/3 season

"I was the best manager in Britain because I was never devious or cheated anyone. I'd break my wife's legs if I played against her, but I'd never cheat her.**"**

Bill Shankly

"Some people believe football is a matter of life and death. I am very disappointed with that attitude. I can assure you it is much more important than that.**"**

(33)

Bill Shankly

❝It wasn't her wedding anniversary, it was her birthday, because there's no way I'd have got married in the football season. And it wasn't Rochdale. It was Rochdale Reserves. **❞**

Bill Shankly

refuting stories that he had taken his wife Nessie to watch Rochdale on their wedding anniversary

"Some people might think we are lazy, but that's fine. What's the point of tearing players to pieces in the first few days? We never bothered with sand dunes and hills and roads; we trained on grass, where football is played.**"**

Bill Shankly

on pre-season trainnig

"Take that bandage off, and what do you mean you've hurt your knee? It's Liverpool's knee!**"**

Bill Shankly

to an injured Tommy Smith

" Now, boys, Crerand's deceptive, he's
slower than you think. **"**

Bill Shankly

preparing for a meeting with Paddy Crerand and Manchester United

“I want to build a team that's invincible, so they'll have to send a team from Mars to beat us.**”**

Bill Shankly

❝ Liverpool was made for me and
I was made for Liverpool. **❞**

Bill Shankly

L.F.C.

CHAPTER 3

RED STARS

"Look, , if you're in the penalty area and aren't quite sure what to do with the ball, just stick it in the net and we'll discuss your options afterwards. "

42

Bill Shankly

gives some pre-match advice to Ian St John

“With him at centre-half, we could play
Arthur Askey in goal!**”**

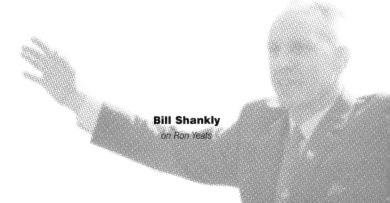

Bill Shankly
on Ron Yeats

44

" Tommy Smith wasn't born, he was quarried. **"**

David Coleman

❝We knew that all other things being equal, like skill, tactics and run of the ball, it was fitness that would count in the end. So we kept at 100 per cent at all times, and it paid us. We have found that there is more satisfaction in a good win than there is in a pint or a cigarette packet.**❞**

(45)

Roger Hunt

He's just stepped out of the shower. Come in and see him…have a walk round him. He's a colossus.

Bill Shankly

unveiling 6ft 2in, 14-stone centre-half Ron Yeats to journalists

"Bill was so strong it was unbelievable. You couldn't shake him off the ball. He could go round you, or past you, or even straight through you sometimes.**"**

Bob Paisley

on Billy Liddell

YOU'LL NEVER WALK ALONE

LIVERPOOL
FOOTBALL CLUB

EST·1892

48

"Yes, he misses a few.
But he gets in the right place
to miss them.**"**

Bill Shankly

on Roger Hunt

❝Keegan had a Doncaster childhood and a Scunthorpe upbringing, yet he seems to have been born with Liverpool in his soul.**❞**

Joe Mercer

"He was never the most gifted player, but I've never known anyone work so hard at his game. He made himself great.**"**

John Toshack

on Kevin Keegan

" Strikers are selfish, at least the very best are. It's not about giving everyone else a chance as far as you are concerned. You want to be out there on the pitch scoring goals. It proves you are a winner. **"**

(51)

Ian Rush

66 He was like a fox in that area, the way he hunted for his goals. **99**

Gérard Houllier

after Robbie Fowler's hat-trick against Aston Villa in 1998

❝Who can say what he's
going to do? It's a talent and you
can't teach it, you can't coach it.
All you can do is enjoy it. **❞**

Roy Evans

discussing a young Robbie Fowler

"I always have my packet of
chocolate buttons. **"**

54

Peter Beardsley
explaining the secret of his success

“ A good skipper, but he could
have been a really great one if he
had been a bit more extrovert. **”**

Bob Paisley

summing up Alan Hansen

"He is the target for all the hitmen in the game. He is the man they are after, yet few of them can kick him out of the game.**"**

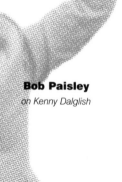

Bob Paisley
on Kenny Dalglish

❝Robbie Fowler's from the South End of Liverpool, like myself. People from that part of the world need to be tough to survive and make a name for themselves. And believe me, Robbie is tough.**❞**

John Aldridge

❝When I sit here in four years I will say we won one title. If not, next time I will manage in Switzerland. **❞**

Jurgen Klopp

on Liverpool FC's title hopes

"He's a walking advert for the benefits of junk food. He'll eat five packets of crisps and wash it down with Coke and Mars bars.**"**

Mark Lawrenson
weighs up Steve Nicol's diet

YOU'LL NEVER WALK ALONE

LIVERPOOL
FOOTBALL CLUB

EST·1892

❝He was struggling… he was probably too unselfish at the time. That's often the case with a young player, particularly one coming into a successful side. He tended to look for others and lay the ball off when he could have had a go himself. I told him to be a bit more selfish, and it wasn't long before the penny dropped.**❞**

Bob Paisley

recalling Ian Rush's goal drought when he first arrived at Anfield

> **❝**I'm referred to more as an ex-Liverpool player than I am any other club. The Liverpool experience is, to use the cliché, never walking alone. It never leaves you.**❞**

David James

66 People don't realise that getting married, which Robbie did in the summer, and becoming a family man can affect you. It's a hell of a transition which can have dramatic consequences. I remember Bob Paisley used to say you would have to forget players for up to 12 months if they had just got married and had children. **99**

Ian Rush

62

❝I never saw anyone in this country to touch him. I can think of only two who could go ahead of him – Pelé and possibly Cruyff.**❞**

Graeme Souness
on Kenny Dalglish

64

“Sometimes I feel I'm hardly wanted in this Liverpool team. If I get two or three saves to make I've had a busy day.**”**

Ray Clemence

❝Steven Gerrard is Souness
with pace and that's a hell of a player. **❞**

Alan Hansen

YOU'LL NEVER WALK ALONE

LIVERPOOL
FOOTBALL CLUB

EST·1892

" If you ask any of the lads, I think
I can have a laugh just like any
other 20-year-old. But at certain times
I think you've got to be serious and
have your head screwed on. **"**

Michael Owen

"Our goalkeeping coach,
Joe Corrigan, has done a fantastic job
on David's mental side. Though you'll never
get that part completely right, because all
keepers are mental anyway.**"**

Roy Evans

on David James

"Footballers are recognised everywhere we go. We were in Dublin once, just doing a bit of shopping, and were mobbed in the street. It was like a scene out of a Beatles movie; we had to run to jump into a cab to escape. Another time I was even recognised on the Great Wall of China!**"**

Steve McManaman

❝ McManaman was a very deceptive player and to see him move on the field you wouldn't think he was travelling as fast as he was. It was only when you saw him outstrip people that you realised how fast he was. **❞**

Eric Sutcliffe

former Secretary of the Liverpool Schools FA

YOU'LL NEVER WALK ALONE

LIVERPOOL
FOOTBALL CLUB

EST·1892

❝I hate training, I hate running, but at Liverpool they say: if you don't put it in at training, how do you expect to put it in during a match?**❞**

Robbie Fowler,
1996

66 Great playing with him, horrible against. **99**

Emile Heskey

pays tribute to Steven Gerrard

" Incey keeps you on your toes because he never stops moaning. **"**

Jamie Redknapp

about his former midfield partner Paul Ince

❝I used to hate Ian Rush when I was
young, because I was a devout Evertonian
in those days, and he seemed to score
every time Liverpool played against us.
He was brilliant to me at Anfield,
always giving me good advice. **❞**

Robbie Fowler

"He can pass, he can tackle, he can do almost anything you put to him. The manager at Liverpool keeps telling him he can get better. If he can, he'll be a frightening sight.**"**

Peter Crouch
on Steven Gerrard, September 2006

(74)

" Is he the best in the world?
He might not get the attention of
Messi and Ronaldo but yes,
I think he might be. **"**

Zinedine Zidane

on Steven Gerrard, March 2009

CHAPTER 4

THE KOP
ON TOP

"The support of the people in Anfield was incredible. Sometimes I'd go there and think: 'Uff! There's a game today.' You might not be in the best mood or be up for the match, but then we'd go out to warm up and it would totally change my mentality. I'd be thinking to myself: 'I have got to score two or three today.'**"**

Luis Suárez

"For those of you watching in black and white, Liverpool are the team with the ball."

Liverpool Fans' *joke before the 1984 Milk Cup final with Everton*

"The Kop was the best place in the world to watch football as you were surrounded by so many characters and passionate people. There used to be a bloke called 'the Mad Brickie' who kept us all entertained by getting on the pitch at half-time.**"**

Ricky Tomlinson

" The Kop's exclusive, an institution,
and if you're a member of the Kop you
feel you're a member of a society, you've
got thousands of friends around you
and they're united and loyal. **"**

Bill Shankly

❝That first night was the greatest. We were in the front row of the Kemlyn stand. The whole time my eyes were fixed on the Kop. I couldn't believe it. I was mesmerised. The steam was rising and the noise was incredible. **❞**

Phil Thompson

remembering his first visit to Anfield at the age of 11

" The whole of my life, what they wanted was honesty. They were not so concerned with cultured football, but with triers who gave one hundred per cent. **"**

(83)

Bob Paisley

on the Kop

"Tell me ma, me ma,
To put the champagne on ice,
We're going to Cardiff twice,
Tell me ma, me ma.**"**

Liverpool fans

*to the tune of 'Que Sera' in celebration of their return trip to the
Millennium Stadium for a Cup Final during the historic
Treble season of 2000–01*

When the ball's down the Kop end, they frighten the ball. Sometimes they suck it into the back of the net.

(85)

Bill Shankly

"I would just love to have gone and stood in the Kop.**"**

Kenny Dalglish

"You had to be strong to be on the Kop. When I was about 13, I tried to go in the middle where all the excitement was and almost got cut in half. I was only 5ft 7in. A big docker pushed the crowd back and I ducked out and went back to my usual place to the left of the goal.**"**

Elvis Costello

❝There's no noise like the Anfield
noise and I love it! **❞**

Ian St John

The highlight of the game was not our two goals or the three points we won. It was when our fans made the Kop sing 'You'll Never Walk Alone'. It was as if they couldn't come here and go home without hearing it sung in all its glory. It was very emotional, and something I'll remember forever.

Kevin Keegan

after Newcastle's 2–0 win at Anfield, 1994

66 It really is amazing to hear your name being sung by all the Liverpool fans. When I heard the chants and saw them waving a flag for me, I was so happy that it gave me goosebumps. **99**

Philippe Coutinho

❝I scored at the Kop end on my home debut and almost finished it off today. I've had lots of great times and have lots of great memories and that is down to Liverpool Football Club and the supporters who have dragged us over the line many times.**❞**

Jamie Carragher

after his final game in May 2013, a 1-0 win over QPR

CHAPTER 5

INSIDE THE BOOT ROOM

66 I remember Jimmy Adamson crowing after Burnley had beaten us that his players were in a different league. At the end of the season they were. **99**

Bob Paisley

“Sometimes if you spit up in the air, it can come back in your face.**”**

Gérard Houllier

reacting to jibes from Crystal Palace's Clinton Morrison after the first leg of the 2001 Worthington Cup semi-final

"He was only an ordinary sized man, but he just had this presence, he used to stand so tall. When he stood in front of the Kop he had thousands in the palms of his hands. **"**

Ricky Tomlinson

in praise of Bill Shankly

" Bill Shankly is as firm as his handshake and that's a real finger-crusher. "

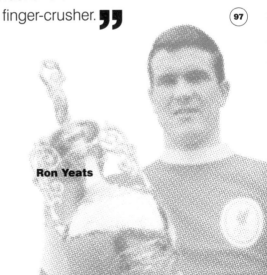

Ron Yeats

"They say he's tough, he's hard, he's ruthless. Rubbish, he's got a heart of gold, he loves the game, he loves his fans, he loves his players. He's like an old collie dog, he doesn't like hurting his sheep. He'll drive them. Certainly. But bite them, never.**"**

Joe Mercer

on Bill Shankly

" If Bill had one failing, it was the
fact that he did not like to upset
players that had done so well for him.
He was a softie at heart. **"**

(99)

Bob Paisley

I'm a totally normal guy. I come from the Black Forest. I'm the Normal One.

Jürgen Klopp

❝I love challenges. I like the aggravation that goes with football management.**❞**

Graeme Souness

taking over at Anfield, 1991

(102)

> **This guy is a living legend. He helps players settle in, young players. He takes them under his wing. His stature and his demeanour will be very difficult to replace but we have to. It will take time.**

Daniel Sturridge
on Steven Gerrard

❝I have only felt like this once before,
and that was when my father died,
because Bill was like a second
father to me. **❞**

Kevin Keegan

hearing of Bill Shankly's death

" When Bob appeared on television the public saw this guy with the wide grin on his face and that quaint Geordie accent which I could never really understand. He was like everybody's favourite uncle. But there was a completely ruthless streak in Bob. If he decided that a player had to be axed, then that was that. Sentiment did not come into it. **"**

Alan Hansen

"I spent the first year on a good horse,
but I was like an apprentice riding the Derby
favourite. I was cautious and went too wide
round the bends. We should have won
the Championship.**"**

Bob Paisley

"He was a great man.
His motion could move mountains.**"**

Ron Yeats's

tribute to Bill Shankly

“Bill Shankly set such a high standard. Liverpool have been geared to this sort of thing for 15 years. I have just helped things along.**”**

Bob Paisley

winning his first title

"He's broken that silly myth that nice guys don't win anything.**"**

Brian Clough

assessing Bob Paisley's triumphs

❝ He, Joe Fagan and Ronnie Moran give the club that homely appearance, but beneath what might seem a soft exterior there is a hard centre. **❞**

Jimmy Armfield

considering Bob Paisley's inner steel

"I never wanted the job in the first place."

Bob Paisley

❝ I'm too old and tired. It's a job for a young man's brains and energy. It's not an eight-hours-a-day-job, it's twenty-four hours a day. And there's no way you can get away from that. **❞**

64-year-old **Joe Fagan**
stepping down as manager

66 Our job is to make the fans happy. When we win, 45,000 people go home happy. When we lose, it not only affects them, it affects the cat. **99**

Gérard Houllier

❝It's like any relationship. Sometimes it goes wrong and you simply have to work at putting it right again. There's no point trying to pretend it's perfect all the time. We don't sit here holding hands seven days a week.**❞**

Roy Evans

on his partnership with Gérard Houllier

❝In Germany I look like everyone else. I'm not the best shaver in the world, funny hairstyle, glasses. **❞**

(114)

Jürgen Klopp

“Reputations do not mean anything
to me. If they did, I would choose Ian Rush
and Roger Hunt up front.**”**

Gérard Houllier

❝Shankly gave the players and the city their pride and passion back. If you didn't have the pride and the passion, then you didn't play for Shankly and you didn't play for Liverpool.**❞**

Fan **Ricky Tomlinson**

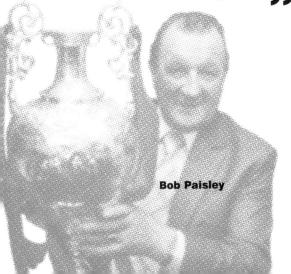

❝ It's not about the long ball or the short ball, it's about the right ball. **❞**

(117)

Bob Paisley

"Even Ian Callaghan had to bend down to get through the door after one of Shankly's team talks. It was amazing how he could build you up.**"**

Ron Yeats

"We didn't know what he was talking about half the time but we knew what he wanted.**"**

Tommy Smith

trying to follow Bob Paisley's mangled English

“Bob would call us together on a
Friday morning and usually just say
'The same team as last week',
and we would get on with it. **”**

Mark Lawrenson

"I don't know what will happen when he goes full-time!"

(121)

Bobby Robson

on Kenny Dalglish's success as player/manager, 1988

(122)

"What do I say to them in the dressing-room? Nothing really. Most of the time I don't even know what they are going to do myself.**"**

Kenny Dalglish

There is no way a game of football is more important than grieving.

(123)

Kenny Dalglish

puts things into perspective after leaving Craig Bellamy out of the side on hearing of fellow Welshman Gary Speed's tragic death

❝If Shankly was the Anfield foreman, Paisley was the brickie, ready to build an empire with his own hands.❞

Tommy Smith

"I don't believe everything Bill (Shankly) tells me about his players. Had they been that good, they'd not only have won the European Cup but the Ryder Cup, the Boat Race and even the Grand National. **"**

Celtic Boss **Jock Stein**

❝Shanks was the father figure but Roger Hunt was something special. It might sound daft but just picking up his sweaty kit gave me satisfaction.**❞**

Phil Thompson

ffYou know I could have stayed in my comfortable chair in South Wales having the first Welsh team that got promoted and been there a number of years, but for me I wanted to work at a club that was world class and at the very, very top. **JJ**

Brendan Rodgers

CHAPTER 6

COMINGS AND GOINGS

"When I went to see the chairman to tell him, it was like walking to the electric chair.**"**

Bill Shankly

on his decision to quit

" I've been blown away by the send-off
I've been given by the supporters and I'd
like to thank every one of you. It's been very
humbling and it's something I'll cherish for
the rest of my life. It's been an absolute
privilege to represent this football club
for so long. **"**

Steven Gerrard's
open letter to fans after playing his last game for the club

❝Don't you recognise him? This man is the future captain of England.❞

Bill Shankly

to a traffic policeman who had stopped him on his way back
to Liverpool with new signing, Emlyn Hughes

"We got him from Home Farm, the boys' club in Dublin, and I think the lads who come to you from that sort of background in the game are the best type. You get England schoolboys and their heads are away before they arrive at the club. I think the failure rate is about 96 per cent.**"**

Bob Paisley

announcing the arrival of Ronnie Whelan

"Kenny Dalglish was the reason I signed for Liverpool. It was his reputation and his stature in the game that persuaded me and the fact that he gave me a particularly smart pair of boots. It is the only 'bung' I have ever received. They were two sizes too big for me, but I didn't half look good in them.**"**

Steve McManaman

❝ He [Bellamy] was unbelievable.
If Man City have anyone else like
Craig that they don't want to keep,
they know where we are. **❞**

Kenny Dalglish

after Bellamy's goal beat City in the 2012 Carling Cup semi-final

"When you come for the first time in a new house, normally you have a present. I am not quite satisfied with my present tonight but it was only the first time and I will come again. **"**

Jürgen Klopp

after his first game in charge at Anfield ended in a 1-1 draw

"Playing Roma in Rome in the
European Cup final and scoring a
penalty in the shoot-out to help us win it.
That was my very last kick for Liverpool
and it doesn't really get any better
than that.**"**

Graeme Souness

❝I may have left Liverpool but the city and club will always be part of me.**❞**

Kenny Dalglish

in 1991

“The chief executive, Peter Robinson, and I had just sat down at our fortnightly meeting with the manager when he came out and said he wanted to finish. I jokingly said: 'This afternoon?' and he said: 'Yes'. **”**

Liverpool chairman **Noel White**

reeling from Kenny Dalglish's shock departure

"Some friends asked:
'Why are you moving to
Liverpool when you play for
Bayern Munich?' Now they realise
it was a great opportunity.**"**

Markus Babbel

❝He is the best player that
Liverpool have signed this century.
It was the best decision we have ever made.
He sets such a fine example, not just to our
players but to everybody in the game.**❞**

Chairman **John Smith**

praising Kenny Dalglish as Liverpool clinch the League title in 1986

"Are we talking about a change of religion here or just a change of football club?**"**

Gérard Houllier

over fears that Nick Barmby may have had to go into
hiding following his move across Stanley Park

❝I'm delighted that he has signed.
I think he's one of the top strikers
in world football.**❞**

Brendan Rodgers

on Luis Suarez, after the Uruguayan entered into a new long-term
contract following the London 2012 Olympic Games football tournament

"Son, you'll do well here as long as you remember two things. Don't over-eat and don't lose your accent. **"**

Bill Shankly

welcoming Ian St John to Anfield

❝I have always wanted to come back and it has been a long time but I'm glad to say I'm back now. Leaving was probably one of my biggest regrets I have had in football. I'm chuffed to bits. I can't really believe it's happened again so I'm ecstatic.**❞**

Kop favourite **Robbie Fowler**
rejoins Liverpool, January 2006

L.F.C.

CHAPTER 7

SECRETS OF SUCCESS

❝Tommy Smith would start
a riot in a graveyard.**❞**

Bill Shankly

❝When you see Tommy Smith go down,
then you know he's been hurt. **❞**

Bob Paisley

(150)

"We do things together. I'd walk into the toughest dockside pub in the world with this lot because you know that if things got tough, nobody would 'bottle' it and scoot off.**"**

Emlyn Hughes
on his Liverpool team-mates

" If I told people that the secret of Liverpool's success is a dip in the Mersey three times a week, I not only reckon they'd believe me but I think our river would be full of footballers from all over the country. **"**

(151)

Club trainer **Ronnie Moran**

"There's so many clubs been ruined by people's ego. The day after we won our first European Cup, we were back at this club at 9.45 in the morning, talking about how we would do it again, working from that moment, because nobody has the right to win anything they haven't earned.**"**

Bob Paisley

66 Bottle is a quality too, you know. It's not just about ball control and being clever. Sometimes you have to show the world what's between your legs. **99**

Graeme Souness

(154)

❝I love tackling. It's better than sex. A great tackle gets everybody pumped up. **❞**

Paul Ince

I always say a squad is like a good meal. I'm not a great cook, but a good meal takes a wee bit of time. But also, to offer a good meal, you need good ingredients.

Brendan Rodgers

"I'm not allowed to wear gloves. When I was about 12, my dad came to watch me play. I brought a pair of gloves out and he walked off!**"**

Steven Gerrard

❝He's brilliant, he's full throttle. He's a genuine guy, his training is great each day and as you have seen on the sideline he is a bit crazy.**❞**

Jon Flanagan

on Klopp

CHAPTER 8

MAGIC
MOMENTS

"We wore the all red strip for the first time. Christ, the players looked like giants. And we played like giants. **"**

Bill Shankly

after Liverpool had worn their all-red kit for the first time, against Anderlecht at Anfield, 25 November 1964

" Getting the Nou Camp booing their own players because they didn't touch the ball in the first ten minutes. **"**

(161)

Emlyn Hughes

recalling his favourite moment from Liverpool's triumphant 1976
UEFA Cup run – a semi-final trip to Barcelona

> **"**This is the greatest night in Liverpool's history. This is the result of planning, of simplicity, of how to play the game in a simple manner. I think the whole world realises that it's the way to play.**"**

Bill Shankly

after watching the 1977 European Cup final

❝I was really confident. I took a penalty in training and put it in the same spot. Just like that.**❞**

Alan Kennedy

after scoring the winning penalty in the
European Cup Final shoot-out against Roma in 1984

"As the ball came over, I remembered what Graham Taylor said about my having no right foot, so I headed it in. **"**

John Barnes
scoring against Taylor's Aston Villa in a 1988 FA Cup tie

"When you play in a European final,
you are looking for immortality. People
remember who was playing and when you
look at programmes from finals you just
recall the facts of the game. These boys
have produced a game which will be
remembered for a long time.**"**

Gérard Houllier

after the 2001 UEFA Cup final

"For far too long our fans have had to see a team in the backwaters of English football, so it is great to have people talking about Liverpool again.**"**

Phil Thompson

celebrating the 2001 treble

"I think the game will be a dull 0–0."

Jordi Cruyff

of Alaves before the UEFA Cup Final

which Liverpool won 5–4, May 2001

"It's best being a striker. If you miss five then score the winner, you're a hero. The goalkeeper can play a blinder, then let one in and he's a villain. **"**

Ian Rush

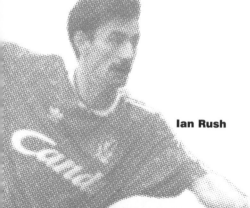

> **"**I just wanted to jump into the stand
> and start celebrating with those
> wonderful fans. **"**

Steven Gerrard

on overcoming Chelsea in the 2005 Champions League semi-final

> **❝** Liverpool produced one of the greatest comebacks in the history of football. They created for themselves an utter disaster and somehow turned a lost match around in six impossible minutes… The tide turned in a manner that defied logical and even tactical sense. It was simply as if God had changed sides. **❞**

Simon Barnes

in The Times on the 2005 Champions League Final

> **"**I saw nothing. Usually I have a second pair, but I couldn't find them. It's really difficult looking for glasses without glasses.**"**

Jürgen Klopp

after his glasses were smashed during last-minute goal celebrations in a 5-4 win at Norwich

"Carra came up to me like he was crazy. He grabbed me and said, 'Jerzy, Jerzy, Jerzy – remember Bruce [Grobbelaar]? He did crazy things in 1984. You have to do the same.' He told me I would be the hero.**"**

Jerzy Dudek

on what he called his 'starfish with jelly legs' routine during the
Champions League Final penalty shoot-out

172

"We talked at half-time and told the players that we needed to believe. We started to press with more energy and the belief came back. I was so proud of my players in extra-time – this was the greatest night I've had as a manager. **"**

Rafa Benítez

❝I'm on top of the world.
This is the best night of my life.**❞**

Steven Gerrard
after holding aloft the European Cup, May 2005

❝I just can't believe the
scenes around here.**❞**

Anfield steward **Phil Lye** *on the Champions League victory as a
man in his twenties, naked but for a pair of socks and a large flag, was seen
running along the streets of terraced houses near the stadium info*

MAGIC MOMENTS

❝It was difficult to say we deserved to win or the other team. It was a magnificent Final. **❞**

Rafa Benitez
celebrates lifting the FA Cup, after a penalty shoot-out, May 2006

“I don't know when the last time we were there was, but we know where we are going. We've maybe forgotten the route because we've not been there for a while, but I'm sure the driver will remember.**”**

Kenny Dalglish

relishing Liverpool's first trip to Wembley since 1996

(178)

❝Steven Gerrard could play right-back and still be effective because these are world-class players. I wish he had been at right-back though!**❞**

Burnley boss **Owen Coyle**

after seeing his side hammered by Liverpool, September 2009

" Well, the bell might not quite be tolling for Real Madrid, but there is a man wearing earplugs preparing to climb the tower. **"** (179)

ESPN commentator **Adrian Healey**

as Liverpool overwhelm Real 5–0 on aggregate, March 2009

❝I kicked every ball tonight. I'm more tired now than when I play! **❞**

Injured **Steven Gerrard**

after watching the 4–4 draw with Arsenal in a TV studio, April 2009

❝I think anyone who has ever won a trophy, whether it's at Wembley or wherever, has come away and said, 'I enjoyed that, I'd love to do it again'. **❞**

Kenny Dalglish, *after Liverpool had won the Carling Cup, 2012*

CHAPTER 9

YOU'LL NEVER
WALK ALONE

" I've been on this planet for 45 years, and have supported Liverpool for 42 of them. **"**

Roy Evans

becoming manager in 1994

"The only thing I fear is missing an open goal in front of the Kop. I would die if that were to happen. When they start singing 'You'll Never Walk Alone', my eyes start to water. There have been times when I've been crying while I've been playing.**"**

Kevin Keegan

❝ I've always said that you can live without water for many days, but you can't live for a second without hope. **❞**

(186)

Brendan Rodgers

" Nothing had changed in my routine,
except that when I went down the chippy
and got me special fried rice, it would be
wrapped in a newspaper that had my picture
all over it. **"**

(187)

Robbie Fowler

If we had to lose our record, I'd sooner it be against Liverpool than anyone else.

(188)

Newcastle boss **Kevin Keegan** *as Liverpool became the first team that season to take a point at St James' Park, 1994*

YOU'LL NEVER WALK ALONE

❝Worldwide, Liverpool's a club that
is renowned throughout. I think you go
to wherever, Kuala Lumpur, New Zealand,
as far away as you can, everyone knows
about Liverpool.**❞**

Brendan Rodgers, *just before his first*
Merseyside derby, 2012

❝Think my chances of making
the Liverpool side are gone now.
Might still be able to get a game
at one of those London
clubs though. **❞**

Liverpool fan **John Peel**

at his 50th birthday party

❝I love the club, the fans and the city and, with a club like this and supporters like this, I could never say no to staying.**❞**

(191)

Rafa Benítez

committing himself to Liverpool until 2014

" Walk on, walk on,
With hope in your heart,
And you'll never walk alone,
You'll never walk alone. **"**

The Kop Choir, *every home game from 1963
to the present day*